Airstream Land Yacht

AIRSTREAM

LAND YACHT

KEN BABSTOCK

Edie,
Best to you
Ken Babstock

ANANSI

Published in 2006 by
House of Anansi Press Inc.
110 Spadina Avenue, Suite 801
Toronto, ON, M5V 2K4
Tel. 416-363-4343
Fax 416-363-1017
www.anansi.ca

Distributed in Canada by
HarperCollins Canada Ltd.
1995 Markham Road
Scarborough, ON, M1B 5M8
Toll free tel. 1-800-387-0117

Distributed in the United States by
Publishers Group West
1700 Fourth Street
Berkeley, CA 94710
Toll free tel. 1-800-788-3123

House of Anansi Press is committed to protecting our natural environment. As
part of our efforts, this book is printed on paper that contains 100%
post-consumer recycled fibres, is acid-free, and is processed chlorine-free.

13 12 11 10 09   3 4 5 6 7

LIBRARY AND ARCHIVES CANADA CATALOGUING IN PUBLICATION DATA
Babstock, Ken, 1970 –
Airstream land yacht / Ken Babstock.

Poems.
ISBN 978-0-88784-740-0

I. Title.

PS8553.A245A64 2006   C811'.54   C2005-907390-X

Library of Congress Control Number: 2006920155

Cover design: Bill Douglas at The Bang
Text design and typesetting: Ingrid Paulson

 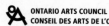

Canada Council   Conseil des Arts   ONTARIO ARTS COUNCIL
for the Arts   du Canada   CONSEIL DES ARTS DE L'ONTARIO

We acknowledge for their financial support of our publishing program the
Canada Council for the Arts, the Ontario Arts Council, and the Government of Canada
through the Book Publishing Industry Development Program (BPIDP).

Printed and bound in Canada

To Laura

CONTENTS

LAND

YACHT

Theory of Mind

Milk of input. Milk of matter.
Honeyed *epoché*.
Honey of all
that seems to me to be—

But when our *billy bee*'s half empty,
we can see straight through his head!

AIR

The scholar of one candle sees
An Arctic effulgence flaring on the frame
Of everything he is.
—WALLACE STEVENS

Essentialist

Snug underground in the civic worm burrowing
            west, I was headed to class when a cadet
                in full combat dress got on my train.

                But for a pompom sprucing up the beret,
            his age, the fact he was alone, and here,
this boy could've been boarding amphibious

landing craft. I checked for guns, grew pious
            of this spinning orb's hotter spots. He
                was all camo, enactment-of-shrubbery, semblance

                of flora in varying shades, hues, mottlements
            of green. A helmet dangled on his back, a hillock
in spring, sprouting a version of verdant grasses

in plastic. I got past enjoying a civilian's recoil
            from things military, brutal, conformist, and took
                a peek at what my soldier was so engrossed in—

                Thoreau's *Walden*—imagine him, rubbing oil
            into a Sten gun's springed bolts, working through
his chances at a life away from men: berries

plumping in among their thorns, night's
            curtain drawn across the window of the lake...
                We must reconcile the contradictions as we

                can, but their discord and their concord
            introduce wild absurdities into our thinking
and speech. No sentence will hold the whole

truth, and the only way in which we can be just
         is by giving ourselves the lie; speech is better
                  than silence; silence is better than speech;—

         All things are in contact; every atom has
      a sphere of repulsion;—Things are, and are
not, at the same time;—and the like. There are other

minds. Surfacing at St. George, I cupped my hands
        and blew—bodies scattering among museums,
            bank towers, campus rooms, and shops, each

            to where they're thinking of or not, seemed
        to prove a law we're locked into, demonstrable
with iron filings, magnets, and clean tabletop.

I can watch their faces go away. The singing's not
        to record experience, but to build one viable
           armature of feeling sustainable over time.

           The stadium's lit, empty, and hash-marked
        for measuring the forward push. On the surface
of the earth are us, who look in error, and only seem.

Aurora Algonquin

Evidence of a wolf pack's passing marred the otherwise clean
snow basin of the park's Barron Canyon: their in-line
one-two-one's a juddering paragraph of morse—
They'll run a deer down this whitened concourse,

surround and pin it to a cliff face,
or let its own weight send it through thin ice.
I, or the vodka, stood recalling Mr. Marysak explaining
in Geography, rock's rust-red tint as proof of iron-rich

seams when the pinned-up cowl or hood of stars
didn't collapse exactly but popped or blew a stitch;
a familiar seepage in weak-lit jades deepened, altered course

to crimson, and fell in successive tides from directly overhead
till that night entire became a darkroom developing
its notion of a thing outside the visible: pure in deed, and fed.

Windspeed

We were more than a little sullen on the descent—
ticked, really, at the dead-calm state of the air
at the summit of Topsail. Like a row of penitents,
we'd hiked the hard-scrabble straight up, lugging beer

and a designer kite. It was blue and red and meant
to funnel gusts through its windsock frame. Far
from catching a mean updraft, it spent
the afternoon nose down in the crowberries and fir.

What monarch butterfly in Sumatra was so spent,
so drugged or lifeless it couldn't flap one ear-
shaped wing just once and cause a breeze, at least a dent
in the Wedgwood stillness we stood inside up there?

We coiled it and came down. And down on the crescent
of shale, four different kids tugged on the guide wire
of four different kites and hollered and bent
backwards at the strength of their flight. Composure

legged it back to the truck, we lit smokes and began to vent
into our chests. Colin moved first, sidling over near
a glib little pilot and flicking open a Leatherman blade. I went
with it, thumbing the grind-wheel of my Zippo under

the thin string nearest me. It left as if snipped. A parent
saw what his boy had lost and ran over full of hot air,
clutching tongs that pincer-gripped a heat-split wiener.
We shrugged and sniffed as the appendix of string burnt

to a cinder. We were up in the rarer atmosphere,
the social layer, where it often gets hard to breathe, and silent.
A new constellation just then visible over
Belle Isle, specks leaving, signs enacting what signs meant.

Explanatory Gap

Happiness, happiness, happiness. Happiness. Sound of rabbits
                    freed from the hutch, ass-
upping their way toward the Interstate. Etymology of 'blizzard'
                                        unknown.
I repeated that for weeks when conversations stalled, dried up,
                                            exposed

the embarrassed cracks, or I'd stopped listening. But sure as shit
one among us would get it in her head
to thieve a cache of civic pride

that wasn't ours, then stain the river with it, and we'd be up and
                                                out, hailing
the Jumbotron we'd nailed our eyelids to…ah, Big Face.
Speak when spoken to. It glowed a gory orange at times, the river,
                                            like the bands

of a milk snake, and just thinking of kibble made mid-sized dogs
                                        recall that reek
of acetate. They thought of kibble a lot, back then, the dogs.
Crest and trough and the distance between crests over
                                        a given time span.

Tarantella

Having just watched my dogs suffer their bordatella
winding, having just flashed back to my own spiking, as a girl,
     against rubella,

I was serving him Nutella
on dinky bread, this guy, whose ex once serenaded—and
     beautifully, apparently—a harbour seal with Ella

Fitzgerald songs from a kayak, proffering up strips of fat-striped
     mortadella
and pitted cherries. And from within the darkened crescent my
     patio umbrella

made, I wondered who and why this fella
might up and tell a

girl, a girl already suffering from, like, *l'angoscia del hora della
posta* due to debt racked up with Visa, the library, and a man who
     resembles Danny Aiello,

a thing so intimate as to make her Cosa Bella
itch. And *so soon!* So soon after the portobello

mushrooms had come off the grill a
little darker, crispier than is my usual, ah,

preference. I bought some minutes by casting down my gaze,
     intoning *la illaha illa Allah,*
till he noted no burka, and pressed on, pushing his Costello

frames up with a forefinger, *a barrel, a
steamer trunk, a shipping container couldn't hold what I have to tell you…*

More sure of his own worth was this dude than even Cela,
he could, I decided, fork it in alone, hold forth alone, sit alone at
    his own Valhalla

and spare me the blah and the blah,
so I gathered the dogs and waltzed off to work on my libretto. Tra-la.

Found In a Sock Monkey Kit

Sometimes making is play, only that. I've not been
made yet, but will be, and when willed
into my bean-baggish zen loll

might wish for you nights of no nightmare,
layabouts with or without some other
when words are your mind's lit

carousel, monkey bars, or gravel pit, not the spiral
jetty you like to make of it. We pretended
affection each for the other, then

wrecked the furniture, is what we'll say when
they ask how we spent the duration. Single
man and his simian right hand, *memento*

origo, minister of the bemused stare. Lean me
against the neck of the reading lamp: sleep,
farts, fucks, illnesses, and idleness, I'm *I*

through and through, function removed from the feet
and become face with a grin and stillness,
form that gives if you hold it when there's only you.

Hungerford Note

Lives like ours—patched, derided, thin—
meet more on their going out than on
their coming in. Great gales, maybe, churning

up the sea's winey darkness, dressing
its swells in shreds of froth. Or a single,
very amusing man in waistcoat, doing

amusing things with rubber balls. Careless
tinkling on the chipped keys of a piano stood
upright. An officious-looking document

typed out on parched vellum, demanding
we behave athletically, mutter on
about percentages while the alders flash

their underthings through the overlong and
muggy nights of Arkansas. We *were* shown
the exposed flank of a chance-to-be-otherwise

back when, and when. One of us looked off, one
curled a lip, regarded himself with grave
import while men in weathered coveralls

removed the signs and rolled back the dripping
awnings. Everything closed, remember?
They showed and took away. A purplish resin

spread over evening and we demanded, if
demanding can be said to happen silently,
to know what had been done with our early

efforts all those skunked days in the church
basement. It looked to be worsening off to the west.
I have a photo, somewhere, of you in thinning

corduroy and cotton shirt that bore a number, you
were standing back-on to the smudged lens, your
legs obscured by umbrellas of rhubarb, that white,

dust-like matter afloat in the summer air so I thought
you might sneeze as was like you, we had done
something with the day that limped off behind where

you stood, and now the smells of proximity—I to you
and the reverse—were rent so as to allow in a stinging,
brutish, mind-on-forever sort of what?—

       I'm writing by lamplight. I can hear the trolleys
biting the bones of the street. If you get this before
the onset of winter, think on it. We were very wrong.

Stencil Artist

There was the covert summer fling—
rail bridges, back lanes, blue dust of building

sites—with the NSCAD dropout (b.68, Khanesetake)
who worked at night with stencils and spray

paint, enlivening the poured forms of the capitol
with red and black silhouettes of ordinary people.

Meridians, bank walls, light poles, high rises.
I asked her to outline clearly her emotional boundaries

but at the front edge of fall we had words over colour;
a flare-up, really, over

who was seeing what when they saw what
they claimed. Tempers got hot.

Steady brown hand on a Stanley knife,
she cut me—expertly—out of her life; the life

I see now I'd been
filling in.

I catch glimpses of her anywhere the city is. Or is
that me, dead still, spread thin?

State Your Needs

To eat the pistil and stamen both, of a flower rarer
than kermode bear paw, doesn't travel well at all,

and must be leached of liquid, near Iqaluit, by clean air.
Nice wheels, a sweet ride; a snorting Valiant, Impala,

or Duster. Short of that, a Trabant. A spiritual guide,
like Gibran, but smart; well-packaged, pithy stuff

I already know, for pre-sleep, irony by Ikea-light, to get my
breathing slowed. To appear a little off on *Off*

The Record—Poet and silky striker in rec-league soccer—spouting off,
letting fly, making it clear to Landsberg why we never qualify.

Every distal and proximal cause in full-colour diagram.
A scale model of that bridge in Rotterdam

that spans the Maas. The odd Lorazepam.
To be reunited with that Zippo Jeff had engraved with a K.

A thank-you from the kid found crumpled in a stall
in the Queen Mother who'd been shooting K. A stand-in

Father. To be tutored on the TOE's finer points by Michael Green.
Elbow grease. New joints. The information retention and retrieval

of, like, DFW. There's space yet on the form, but the form is our trouble.
What's on offer is finite. What would you say to a stroll

and a bite? Who's up for pad Thai?

Marram Grass

These boardwalk slats intermittently
visible where the sand, like an hourglass's
pinch, seeps between chinks, free-
handing straight lines that stop without fuss—

then fill again, as the wind wills it.
The beach path cuts through undulate
dune land where wild rose, marram grass
cover the scene like a pelt

of shifting greens, or rippled sea of bent
and tapered stalks. To step off
the path's to severely threaten
what a modest plaque declares 'this fragile balance.' If

my affection's bending toward you seems
or feels ever just a blind, predetermined
consequence of random winds,
think of here: our land's end, streams

of ocean mist weighed down your curls,
spritzed your cheeks and lids, made both
our jeans sag and stick. The shore birds'
reasons blow through us too, but underneath

or way above our range of
understanding…even caring. I'll
pass this sight of you—soggy, in love
with me, bent to inspect and feel

the petals of something tiny, wild, nestled
among the roots and moss—over
the projector of my fluctuating self if ever
life's thin, rigid narrowness

requests my heart be small. You taught
and teach me things. Most alive when grit
makes seeing hard, scrapes the lens
through which what's fixed is seen to weaken.

Palindromic

A patrimony all our own: the hours when we have done nothing…It is they
that form us, that individualize us, that make us *dissimilar.*   —E. M. CIORAN

Christmas alone, by choice, with a tin
    of sardines and bonnie 'prince' billy
sharpening the blade of the cold on
    the whetstone of his voice. A melee

on the morning of the first of the year
    over who should pay what to who
for the nothing we got the night before.
    There'd been *lots* of it, but it amounted to

loss, I guess is what I mean, given the pain
    and embarrassing, hours-long absences
of someone with someone else whose name
    should stay out of this. Fences

went up around friendships. The exacto blade
    in the thermometer kept snapping
off segments till there was nothing save numbered
    hash-marks seen through a static

of frost. I went for a walk in a parka I bought.
    Zipped up; the city as a fuzzy-edged
dream sequence afloat to indicate thought
    in the head of a smiling protagonist. Cadge

a light from a passerby and now your head's
    the lantern from the 28th Canto
shedding light on hell. 'Oh me!' you'd said,
    and no laughter, canned or

otherwise, leavened a life that felt filmic.
       Sometime in March, the plaster over
the tub got pregnant, or Anish Kapoor was snuck
       in to redecorate. Its water burst near

April Fool's and spring arrived stillborn, I was
       reading something that hasn't stayed
with me, when the soldiers arrived with shovels.
       It was Mendelssohn screaming at Stoppard,

I think, or Stoppard screaming back, in the letters
       section of the NYRB, about Housman,
was it? As penned by Stoppard?—whatever,
       I remember an exchange of epithets and now's

a little after the fact seeing as the play itself
       never came. One night in May, a barkeep thought
I looked tired and slipped me a pill: I got soft
       in the neck, large in the thumbs, and a spot

of crimson light sang *Agnus Dei* from the foreground
       of my vision's left field. Wall calendars
were argyle socks; all those X's in rows wrapped around
       June under colour shots of designer blenders.

It was like a training regimen to ensure I'd place last
       in the race to accomplish, accrue, attain,
or think straight for a day and a half. I didn't dust.
       Meeting resistance—a door opens onto more rain—

I'd fall back and regroup, reuse the same ringed tea cup
       and liberate a pack of Dunhill from the long ice age
of the freezer. Watched others watch their Weimaraner pups
       grow to full glamour in the park. Massaged

the kinks of appointments from the hurt muscle of months,
    dredged each nightbottom for spare hours
to stare at. Just a therapist and me and a lot of not much
    to work through, more like locating doors

I might walk through if I'd get up and walk. Hypodermic,
    or fifty candies, or warm bath and a pine box:
repeated it all to myself, but self laughed, knew it was weak
    and would linger. Self trips self then mocks

the starfish of limbs washed up in the gravel, another X-
    brace to hold square a day. I read a novel wherein
many were worse off, so read it again, while flecks
    of grey ash mixed with eczematous snow in

the deep gorge between each page. To open it now's
    like opening a text from the Middle Ages, but
you can't, it's glued shut with dead skin cells and sweat. Sows
    at the Ex in August nonplussed with the crowds at

the gate. Too much lost, in ten minutes, at Crown and Anchor,
    and my house keys freed from a pocket while
upside down in those ergonomic gibbets hung from the Zipper.
    So head down for the night on the deep pile

carpet of clipped-lawn embankment that skirts the expressway.
    Stuff fell in the fall. No one took pictures.
Or painted the scene on wood panel in oil, of the day
    none of my friends and I decided not to go halves

on a driving trip through some of Vermont. I read Frost
    and stayed where I was. Thanksgiving
I thanked someone for the chance to play generous host
    to myself as guest at the bar where, having

been dosed earlier that year, we went back for more.
      By November I was an art installation
begging the question are empty days at the core
      of the question of begging the question.

Borrowed money so's not to be anywhere near Christmas,
      while the snow whitened what no longer
wanted to be looked at. I know now I was missed.
      Then was a different story. I think we're all stronger.

A Brochure

Then the belt of penury tightened further
and whether from hunger
or a need to lash back,
we started dreaming of weeks of slack;

a hammock of days
nailed between trees
rooted in the old loam of obligation.
The names of God all sounded like 'vacation.'

And the trips we summoned shimmered
with a nimbus of the definitively unreal: moored
on the Seine in a houseboat
the best feature of which was the wrought

iron collapsing front gate on the lift
descending to a fully equipped
laundry room.
Earning our rent on a loom,

at our leisure, for a cave
with a/c dug into a cliff at the edge of the Mojave.
A month of Sundays of naps
in New York, NY. The chance to collapse

into ourselves or blow apart during monsoon
season any place monsoons
happen. It was just as she was uttering
'Saturn' that I felt my compass returning

to that cabin capped in thick green felt
I'd seen outside Oslo—
not felt, really, a meadow
doing its placid best as a living quilt.

The earth on the roof. Voles over shingles.
Seven kinds of moss softening the gables.
And inside, each step a ride
on the backs of sea birds to a bed on a floor all sky.

STREAM

The towns where the bus stops are not organized towns at all.
—ALICE MUNRO

As Effected by Klaus Berger's Haircut, Whose Brainwaves His Father Recorded Inventing the EEG

As Dragomoshenko, with arm upraised
Russianly, ordered us
'Take it outside,'
my thoughts caught a bus

from the impending KO
to what must
have appeared to those watching as the backside
of that hill, cliff or bluff

that ascends off Fogo
heaving its mist
and gloom at Reykjavik,
more or less,

but was really nothing more
or less than the tanned hide
I saw stacked
once in a plant in Montreal.

Columns and colonnades
of skid upon skid,
encumbered—betowered?—with
kid or cow

the reek of which made us sick
enough to clang back through
that swing-door jobless,
our new fly-halos

honoured to be along for the ride
back to unemployment's arcadia
and what calumny
might next be used

to cow us into quitting as kids,
and take up a place
in the burgeoning
town

of Burgeo, or Burlington,
or some other coven
of bourgeois ease,
where we might both ease

our gripes out to pasture
and await the imminent
blow to whatever
cranial region induces

the shiver that precedes
the blackness
that's like the blackness
in a Greyhound's

window. No sound, just
the dimensions of that pane
delivering a bust
of you to yourself. 'Have made I myself plain?'

Engineer and Swan

I ought not to have visited this scene of terror, I thought at the time.
Today I think differently. It is a good thing I did. Times and methods
do not change. This was yet another proof. —THOMAS BERNHARD

A *childhood blow; they did thrust forth dragonly*
their cleft heads. Bread morsels were money
and they were the greedy. One charred finger
poked from each throat. They chose to linger

in the lee of a cottonwood; scowling, truculent,
grounded accessory: mere landscape.
A punt
in some impressionist's scene now glides by here,
constructed of light-dapple and smudge. The oar

on this side and this side's oar's double
form an arrow on water pointed at us. Stable,
though, as this picture sounds, the boy on our bank,
between us, remember? feels ill. Is ink.

Paid to safely disassemble a bridge in this park,
I do numbers, draft its replacement. It can't work.

Pragmatist

I was on a tractor in the rain
        when it occurred to me, my paternal
            grandfather was called 'Henry James'

        and cooked meals for men in a coastal
        lumber camp in Bonavista Bay.
The brother of that other James

was William who wrote on matters spiritual
        and hung with John Dewey. Henry
            James Babstock's brother's name was Samuel.

        So this grandfather, who went by 'Pappy,'
        died when I was two. He
was a huge man, gentle, happy,

and given to tossing infants in the air.
        Concerning one's self only
            with the task at hand while temporarily

        ignoring metaphysics has had more
        recent support from the American
thinker Richard Rorty. His name

sounds like a tractor coughing, revving,
        having sat idle in a field in the rain.
            When I was two, and at the zenith

        of one of Henry James's loving pitches—
        up near the ceiling of a white clapboard
house that has since been taken down, or

outdoors above the porch, or 'bridge'
     as he and his wife Alma
          would have called it—I was at the edge

          of something. That descent, and all my
     subsequent nothings and entanglements,
loves, riots, slippages, and cries,

could be felt to have happened inside a quiet
     afterthought; a kind of dimming down
          of who I was when I was him and contained.

          Turn now to a book by William James
     on states of religious experience.
I was pulling a trailer onto which

a friend was loading irrigation pipes.
     He was powerful, and beautiful, yet
          far from me, we finished early to a round

          of applause from a bank of thundercloud
     that had reared up over the cottonwoods.
There's a kind of shroud I pull across my life.

Explanatory Gap

Would Form, Colour, and Motion please report to Area 17
where you'll be met by Memory and Recognition. An unbroken
field of light is uninformative. The cracks,

the jinks, what won't cohere or blend but bends, fissures,
                                                    falls to the field
or becomes figure. A visual percept is degraded light.
We all like to sound important. I was convinced I'd actually loved

by a hot tinny pain spreading downward from the sternum. She
                                        was gone, though,
by the time the evidence appeared, and I'd moll around the train ditch
of an evening, reading German dictionaries and pulling
                                        loosened spikes

from the tie braces, designing industrial versions of croquet.
                                        Home shot:
through the St. Louis Arch to the CN tower. Oil derricks and
                                        wrecking balls.
I had no friends for a time. Whether

it happened or didn't it felt as it did and affected the weather. I
was being fleeced, still I paid
for entertainment. It helped me feel worse, and worse was where

lovely numb wet its tongue. I sucked it like a strip of dripping lamb—

Subject, with Rhyme, Riding a Swell

I moved like winter wheat.

I from dull wind came up and quiet.

I wanted and not large was there there to entreat.

I went myself to a parkbench to feed whatever would eat.

I inner-whistling the dumbnesses fanned hard green bread bits

     low by feet.

I shifted, like carbon, like car horns, like cow's jaw, on the slats

     of the public seat.

I knowing how since long years counted then further and chewed

     till it bled on a cheek.

I as sun's going went thought dim of amphibious lurchings of

     claws on smallthing by brown mule-slow creek.

I numbered while chilling wonders that weren't that seemed that

     sidled up as though to the moorings but hedged and

wouldn't complete.

I tethered there unoptioned stayed to no coming no visit no

     gloried knowing to sing of carried on backward at darkening

like the thing sightlessness wants of its own

and claims unlawfully settling a coming despite—

On the Dream of Union Ceasing

The long dream of Union ceased,
                    and his world uncrinkled.
Horizon a pressed seam from the Space Needle
                    to the mean
maximum berg limit out in the toiling
                    east. It made

him squint. Glaucoma newly
                    scraped. He'd been
stood in place; stood here to be looked at;
                    peered
at; inspected by it. Modelling *it*-ness
                    for Horizon:

                                        I
Was it a Greek who said *begin with*
                    the good? Does this feel good?

                                        II
The kids are waving cutlasses and singing of apocalypse,
                    or watching TV.

                                        III
Walk with me to the liquor store, under
                    the effluent, the badger-face cloud.

                                        IV
In the park near the pump under empires of oak,
                    winter sits folding its linen.

V

An ice cream party and Mozart hymns; to live without
hope, or a table saw.

VI

I saw and was relieved. I saw my relief and left. I left
without seeing what I'd done.

Explanatory Gap

Like I said, important.
Calm your amygdala! Keep up with the furtherance

of what's known as best it can be for now. This spruce
is dripping new growth, little lime-coloured nubbins
in the uncorked sun of a Monday. They now can listen in
$\qquad$ on the harmony

of seizures, all the differing bandwidths holding hands
and hooraying, hell, they can trigger them at will, and will.
And when last you gripped a garter snake by its tail, whipping
$\qquad$ it in circles above you,

offering it a Benthamic view of the bean fields and windbreaks,
$\qquad$ you went home
with the feel of its scales—a muscled dryness you could taste—
$\qquad$ and humped
your bicameral mind to bed to stop the senses mingling.

The Lie Concerning the Work

Most were written at home,
some done away,
a few in a bar,
one inside his head.

Many had a tendency to roam,
some felt grey,
a few went too far,
that last refused to be read.

The Brave

That's not what we liked. It wasn't for us.
It was pinned to a stream. Ear-marked.
The *arriviste* mashed up with the avant-garde.
We didn't go for that. That wasn't us.

It wasn't quite right. Lacked focus.
Might have tickled the kids, the simple,
Or those others on that other coast,
but not us. It wasn't what we liked.

It was riding a riptide of research
from Pittsburgh. Big deal. Where
was the spit, the spark, the goatish
smell of the real? Who could tell air

from gas, music from dirge, dinghy
from ark amid all that saleable merch?
I'm saying we didn't like it.
And we didn't. How much? Not much.

We couldn't get in. There were no
knobs on its doors. Goes to show
some prefer building walls and floors
to keep us here, outside, looking in.

That's not what we liked and we disliked
when we did with some vigour. Active.
Off the couch and out with the X. Heave
to with No, No, No, and especially Not.

If there were a key here I'd make that 'No'
bigger. Is it clear what wasn't on for us?
It's about cutting out rot. About rigour. About
the men in acumen and the small made

smaller. We didn't like it from the get go.
It was under the sheets as boys, now
it's everywhere and not. Not liking's like
affirming we're here while stretching here

to include whatever isn't. And we're right.
Show me something we didn't like and I'll
show you airtight. Excruciatingly tight.
It wasn't for us and won't be. Ever. Trust me.

The Minds of the Higher Animals

are without exception irresponsible. Which
sounds alarming and is, admittedly, an aberration
(perhaps not funny) of a more valid, thinkable notion,
that dolphins, wolves, chimps, etc., flip a switch

in us, casting klieg light on the frightening solitude
engendered by the very Fifties idea—I know—
that we alone are responsible for our own
consciousness. A friend, who'd taken work as tutor

to a high-school student, leaned over the back wall
of a booth in a pub and told me: of all the thumbnail
sketches he'd done for her, from *Plato* to *Pascal*
and beyond, this Sartrean concept of taking ownership over all

that you know, feel, and do, had proved the most opaque,
the singularly *most inconceivable stupidity*
ever designed to befall a girl, driving her to kick some shitty
desk chair in frustrated disbelief. Now, Reader, make

a face that's meant to express some woeful sense
of pity and surprise, while feeling a cold sickness underneath.
That was my face. I was mumbling things so far from the truth
of what I felt, I could have been a clergy entering the manse,

touching tops of heads, asking how days went, seeking food,
while wishing one or the other end of this circus dead.
The sight of a pint glass didn't cause me to vomit. I didn't
reel, sweating and murderous, out into the street; but my mood

stiffened, grew intractable, opaque; I felt blue flashes inside
that were flares of all the moments I'd sought causality,
a why for each failing of character, somewhere outside
of myself, amounting to a web of reflexive sophistry

that reached back into the years of my life like illness
discovered late, or how rot sets into wood compromising
the strength of a structure by softening its centre. Rising
from my seat, I went and faced a woman whose caress

had eased my passage through some months I couldn't pass
through on my own, she'd been more than kind, I'd
found I couldn't love her at the time, and fled.
So I faced her, and apologized as best I could, given the mass

of people in the pub. 'This is a poem,' she said, 'and that's not
good enough. Around here, we don't let art, no matter
how acutely felt, stand in for what's necessary, true, and right.
Next time you face me, maybe leave you here. End quote.'

Epochal

A video loop. A video

loop of a Rhode Island wind inspiriting the natural-colour tresses
                                    of one Bernardine Dorn
as she adjusts the sit of her shades, while the boom
                finds its level, then recounts her decades-
long exploits in
the Weathermen.

An etched plate. A plate

depicting a troop of shades infilling each other's footprints that pass
                                    behind one Bertran de Born
who's clutching his severed melon by its medieval
                tresses while bemoaning, well, plans best-laid.
Something explodes.
Connect them.

Lowlands with Encroaching Sea

Originary cling, muck compress
      on the senses.
Antennaless ant, little miner mole in a cave-in; what
      is consciousness at night?

Irruption, flickering blather, drip-damp
      in the ass cleft,
warbling lullabye as the outline of the hair erases
      a form of hair to begin its

lick at the scalp. Isotherms tauten and snap.
      I know I'm not no-
where: *grease came off the cook pans*
      with sand and a little soap, arenas

are where the unlived live out their tenure
      and flower as bruise, Mons,
mons pubis, I owe the government money, Planck
      Length, V-dub under green water in

the quarry. It needs an outline; I owe the future
      some questions.

Ataraxia

I'd come in from a wind, a wind in a storm with snow
like atomized iron, part chandelier part bomb, it hurt
to inhale. An engorged winter snow that ignored each cardinal
point on the compass, and Newton, and foreground, and
it ignored depth. Snow with layers of enamelled white
degrading through grey to black, black snow that shivered

white again in the acid of stung, underlid vision. Knifed
onto the canvas snow as the canvas creases, then tears.
The tips of two fingers rolled loose in the purse of a glove,
and a dollar-size patch of dead flesh collected crystals
under one eye. Gliding on the stump-end of each femur,
I reeled, gill-snagged by the collusion of wires above

and banged into the barn wood door before the door had gained
outline and was more than the snow shift and ground static.
It gave, and leaked a column that glowed. Air in that lung
was unalive, warm, moted, smoky, how I had imagined air
in my own, before I'd left the great enclosure months hence,
to come here, though at the point of my leaving 'here' was no option.

Then I was sitting, a snow-pack on one hand stalling the thaw,
and chewing hard on my face with weak teeth. Iron pry-bars
and outsized wrenches hung like strips of smoked meat from
spikes in the studs. The studs crowned outward, and cracked
like the whip's end the wind held the handle of, out past
the weakening hydro towers. There were wood chips, a stool,

and a curling portrait of Curtis Strange in his backswing; two
palm leaves browning through the frame of his high arm. Seeing
was shearing browns from the not-there's of black, except where
the heat source bled orange onto the meltwater and ice still
clinging to seams in my gear.

It was here I began hoping the angel
of quiet might visit, gripping the past in its talon; a past devoid

of plastics and canker, shame, stale grievance, Vancouver, debt,
shortfall, and waste—

'You stain what sections of now I've allowed
You,' I said, addressing the past as a pain-fire in the flesh of my feet
took root, 'your slavish insistence on sticking around, on bearing
down on the hours as they enter and be, siphons the glow off your
stardom. You and your retinue reek. I've a chance here to gaze at this

oil can on into tomorrows. Equilibriate. Blot the weather and settle.'
Outside was tearing its fingernails out, eating the elderly in drifts-
become-tombs. The notion of water froze in the mind of outside
and all vertical entities had relinquished pretensions.

'You had
a chance. Then you opened your mouth.' Its voice came from nowhere,
as the past needs nowhere to be, and deadened the details of the things

I could see. 'Your good eye hangs the way it does due to me. Padlocks
in your lower back, and the list of cities that rented you space. The love
defiled by disallowing the ground it grew into. Remember, bored child,
as a flea on the flesh of disquiet, you'd have given fingers to have
things mean, prior to seeing, disturbing, and reading them.' The sun,
a governing body, had entered a phase of secrecy it couldn't discuss.

Or there wasn't a sun.

'Miles of Europe went by, and then it was dark'
—ANDRÉ ALEXIS

Thankfully, he arrived
long after
it was *de rigueur*

to sew insignias
onto sleeves,
or wrap a band

around. For a time
he thought much
of mirrors, doubleness,

Paris, and the Author;
but when he met
one, and shook her hand,

it was warm, she
smelled of lilacs,
exhaled smoke,

and scratched where a bug
had bit her arm.
Was convinced for years

the sign had turned
its face away
from God. It had.

So God switched seats
the better to read,
and now words still mean,

more or less, give or take,
what his COD
says that they mean.

He took a photo
in Berlin of Hegel
on a pedestal;

it was evening, and bluish,
and his face
developed wrong. The flash

made the streaks and stains
of time glow white
and his eyes appeared

as pits. He visited
the very spot
in the North Atlantic

that marked the shift
when Auden went
from there to here.

It was cold, and deep.
He stood and smoked
with an older, wiser

man at the battle-
ments at Cape Spear,
and looked east,

or back towards,
or out past the seam,
or just out, and thought...

nothing, really,
that hadn't already
been, so they talked

about love for a while.
I recieved a card
from him; he's in

Saskatchewan,
learning to farm,
alone, one leg is gone.

LAND

I read today in the *Taganrog Herald* that I am in Kislovodsk. This is not true. I have not been to Kislovodsk this year.
—ANTON CHEKHOV

From Under a Quicklime Veil

The black polyps of bin bags,
      cinched at the stem-end
to an anus, braille the street,
      gleaming in lamplight.

Gasoline fractals proving higher
      maths near the curb. Tight
turns where idlers groan with
      their hazards on, they'll defend

what's theirs and whatever's
      here is theirs: a leather
recliner star-gazing on the free
      side of a yard fence, a desktop

monitor with night scene screen-saver
      thinking dark thoughts
to itself, and love letters on brown
      deli paper by those who,

when they say heart, mean heart.
      A gull feather disguised
as a straw. *World without end*
      arrives through the mailslot

before we wake, decodes, and climbs in.

Explanatory Gap

It was Nineteen-Eighty-BoreYouToDeath and sex had attached
                                          its lips to Things.
New was no longer the inverse but the utter annihilation
of old. New laws, models, growth on the hedgerows
                              that had to be hacked. New

fear: moles with bleeding edges; monkey bars, merry-go-rounds,
                                          outlawed lawn
darts; the poems of ex-presidents; crack, glue, gas, E; evangelists
on their knees, and a funky steam roiling over from the
                                    Unter den Linden.

I hear *Stasi*, I see the *Nordiques*. We can't know what things mean
                                    in the place
where they're meant, or know what's meant by place
with no map in our head. Like those whose hobby

it's become to dog-sled, day-hike, air-lift in to where latitudinal
lines meet the north-south ones at some lonely, never stepped-on
patch of steppe or muskeg mat in Labrador; and they intersect

there, apparently, though there's nothing to see, or nothing
visibly marking the spot other than the spot itself: the mapped
land beneath the numbered globe. Say hello

to coordinates-ordinates-ordnance, and a ground rodent
sniffing the spruce air under a daytime moon.
There'll be a sign here soon.

Mill Town

That? That was our Crowned Selves looking to take
      up office; sit our asses
on thrones of planks, on lake pontoons,

there to wait out Accomplishment in the gummy light.
      Gravel infected the corn-snow drifts
melting over the shoulders

of the drainage ditch. O
      sick piñata. Another's mother spun on her
belt from the basement joists.

Car lot, car lot, et al., matchsticks
      in the millions. We went bored, but our folks went boreder.
That was couldn't tell pill

from pill, or why a baldy
      sun lowered itself in the river, cooling slug, black
smoke sniffing down over

the hills from Quebec, dark blanket, dark
      pillow, dark you wanting a feelable ingrain,
a knot for the incoming awl. That

was the wood in our *Would that I might.*

Materialist

Where I put my palm to the crushed
         granite exterior, to the tooled wood
        of the portico's columns

         banded by afternoon sun, I
        thought I could feel where rain
had earlier that day slickened, cooled

then warming, vanished. There'd been
        an interlude of rain. The sun made
         a cracking sound and resumed breathing.

         Our coats opened. The hemmed
        end of yours clawed a jar of preserves
from its place on a deli shelf. Red Sicily

expanding in a laminate sea. Where Prince
        Arthur leaves the Main, sets and subsets
        of visitors, kids, residents drew Venn

        diagrams around buskers. I went
        toward the gaunt, tinny sound of spoons,
fiddles, expecting farce or illness. About being

loved, and returning love, we'll say it heats
        the surface in its passing, then becomes
        surface, a tactile skin on the world

        our eyes feel in photons, chiasmic
        inversion of what's purportedly there. You
at the edge of the gathering watches

you at the gathering's edge. So it
                  would seem. Montreal; 3 p.m. in the strange
                          warmth, aren't we now hung on the rack

                    of the problem of some smaller 'you'
             happier left—or kept—alone? Tiny mote,
mote's opposite, unmeasured, entirely featureless

but for its property of denied emergence. The music
              fell out of a cheap tape deck. Above that
                  a plaid-shirted marionette clogged away

                  in his scaled-down cabin. Fire flickered
           from a wood stove made of two
thimbles. A rocker set in motion by the footfalls.

Art hung on the walls, and a view onto
             green-blue woods where jays battled
                 the hours away; fire-ditch; spring melt—

                  I was warming to the show, when
            the puppeteer removed his hands, stepped out
and clapped along. Then he left, and it went on.

Late Drive Toward Innisfil

Late morning we arose and went;
West Gwillimbury,
Wooden Sticks, coats of arms carved
into the overpass,
Maples of Ballantrae, and box stores...

a barn wall tagged by the one boy pinned
to the peace on that farm,
an X-Box, culture
in bold colour bleeds into flea markets.
Everyone sweats and crawls north.

This will be our 13th
concession. Purple loosestrife let
loose through Nottawasaga.
New Nevada plates on a purple
Cutlass chewing the scenery.

Patterns are a ruse.
Our dashboard's dark, compartmentalized
life illuminated as the jaw's latch
drops. Little bulb, little bulb over wet naps
and manuals—

So Hush a Mask

It was a stool or a stump I sat upon. The sky
was white. There had been birds
at one point, in the past, now an aluminum quiet could be heard
gnashing through the upper branches. I

liked it. I thoroughly enjoyed it...if that's not
going too far. For a while I thought
of how my own face looked, reflected in the display screen
of an instant teller around midnight; a green

PLEASE INSERT YOUR CARD floating like war paint
just above where my mouth should be. I bored of that soon
and placed the toe of one shoe
on top of the other, which made me feel humble, a bit quaint,

as though I should be shelved next to pillows painted with ducks
and fisherwives smoking pipes
carved out of balsam. When another thought got ripe
I shooed it away before the smell hit. Luck

appeared in the long grass and glistened like Emily's
snake. Would *you* have paid any more
attention, what with such crystalline inner calm? The letter from Bangor,
Wales, waiting to be opened? The families

of raccoons headed to church?
I didn't mean to sound testy; it's just
I've been here a while, and your face had that mild crunch
of disdain—Is that a helicopter? This can't last.

But perhaps can be altered a titch so as to include
more than the principal and his attendant shades. Their mood
dictates when they show or don't so bugger
them if they're not here for the planning stage; bigger

fish to fry, pressing engagements, a man about a cudgel,
all that dreck. So, let's see. Do we
count in the blasted regions east of here where the poor huddle
in their thundering shacks? Do we?

The World's Hub
after Pier Paolo Pasolini

Not poor, but adjacent to that, I lived
in an outer suburb, undistinguished but
for the mauve-blue mirrored panels of glass

alongside the feeder lanes. Not country
and no sort of city. Everyone drove, to all points
within the limits of nowhere; the rest

incarcerated on public transit: packed
in the high-wattage strip light
sat the poor, the mad, the adolescent

and license-suspended, the daylight
drunk, and Malton's newly arrived.
Hours-long treks through air-quality

alerts, fingering vials of hash oil and
transfers back. Or earlier, at the thin edge
of long dusks, the Bookmobile

dripping grease on clean tarmac
nudging the lower leaves of young maples,
I kissed a Jamaican boy with three

names, his loose jheri curls
looked wet and right, black helices
in the bay windows' blue glow.

And something inside me took root;
a thing mine that I didn't own, but cared
for, as I had for a pink-eyed rabbit,

loved without reason and was returned
nothing in kind, and so what? The flurry
of rose-brick façades being raised

on cul de sacs without sidewalks, outlets
and outlets, the sameness, and grimmer storeys
of the projects beyond the ballpark

were a weird history I was casting love
upon even as I wanted to leave it. I worked
retail, weekends, from within an awareness

of myself as Self; the brown carpeted tiers
of the library, ravine parties, parading
my young body through malls. The world's

hub, improbably, here, under untranslatable
verses of powerlines, kestrels
frozen above vast grassland of what used

to be farm. November like a tin sheet
blown up from the lake over Mimico, with
garbage and refuse I'd build

a hilltop to the moon over Mississauga—
chip bags, flattened foil wrappers, shopping
carts growing a fur of frost, the shocking

volume and echo of squat women's voices,
here from blasted South Balkan huts
via Budapest; Filipinos, Croatians

with income come to make good
and did, dressed us in suede pantsuits
at ten, or terry summer halters, confident

with adults, curious, clean. Damp
electrical storms, bloated purgings
of rain turning the avenues to linked lakes.

The low slung buses veering, Albion-bound
but stalled in a monoxide cloud
somewhere on the usual grid...

it was the world's hub.
If you feel otherwise, that it constituted negative
space, I can only say it's a postulate

without need of proof but for the love
I had for it. I knew before I could speak
of it—that great, horrible sprawl

folded under airport turbulence, advancing inland
each year, breeding signposts, arteries, housing—
it was life as it was lived. Raspberries. The smell of gas.

Expiry Date

Notice those days when everything sounds a little lewd? YIELD
signs at hidden corners, *Downtown Rugs*, the word 'oubliette'

appearing innocently enough in an essay on circus workers, yet
when you've chased it down in the COD it's lying under 'ouananiche'

and looming over 'ouch.' When the eye notes that the pop.
of Ouagadougou sits at 690,000 a shower seems in order.

Should there not be a shield, a form of protection the out-there
can employ against the pushy the blue-lensed

the crotch-clutching urgency making a mess of in-here?
We ought to keep it to ourselves; between ourselves;

draw the curtains. Oughtn't we?...Contractions have begun.
Or when Merrill said to Jackson, *this ought to be fun!*

After all, 'Ouija' comes from french 'oui' and German 'ja.'
It's what we think we saw that sticks, never what we see.

Worshipful Company

Nothing under sweats with a drawstring;
bobble-ended, like painted gold tassels
on some archduke's
or king's

portrait. Posed
in a manner suggesting
we wrestle, I focused on those
till their gordian knot reminded me

of nothing so much as whatever hole
I'd been darning with needle
and thread when I froze,
unhinged, got

free unharmed of
the backstitch and thimble
to throw myself at her accessibleness.
I said, 'lo,' and, 'lo,' and, 'your Highness.'

The Nabokov-Wilson Letters

Pursued through Buckhorn,
          Bridgenorth, and Chemong,
by a faceless, fedora'd man
          who watched you shudder and bite down
on your lower lip,
          in the Kawarthas, where we lit
Coleman camp stoves, stripped
          in the river, and brought God near us.
The best lines of that stiff
          correspondence we agreed
were Volodya's.

          But that was it. Generator.
Generator. The crank noise
          blankets the actual, revises
the lived down to the letter.

Franconia

We passed homes half-sheathed in Tyvek,
new model King Cabs guarding the lawns,
their tailights turned to the coughed-out wreck
out back on breeze-blocks. Vermont's gone, gone

over to students swarming the motels. It's
Labour Day weekend, Robert, and we've stopped
at the house on a whim, on our way east,
and I like the road's steep grade, that gravel popped

like gunshot up under the chassis, a sign said 'Park,
Walk the Rest of the Way' or something like that
and a rabbit hutch or root cellar was sinking or sunk
into hosta-shade and soft ground. This is the Adirondacks

nearly a century after your *most obvious bid*
for remembrance, yet, again, war is radically diverting
lives, ending many, seeding hate in the sap of some in its bid
to own them. New Hampshire's hills are sine wave, flow chart,

misted, layered, mallard-green. I can't mention the birches
without them bending, a boy at each tip or as far up
as he could get, now riding his own weight as it searches
for the earth. Here are your readers, then, stealing a nap

in a borrowed Buick, passing dentists on Goldwings
in flight from what's said of their profession, drained,
at day's end, by the seaweed of evening,
afraid to stop, to feel the closed world tick, shiver, mean

one thing or another. Read what in the wood veneer?
Much of this world's a facsimile of one, though
we all must be somewhere, awash in sighs through
the papery walls, drifting into the pain of our neighbour.

Anxiety in Vigelund

The conifers cough and a needle mat grows—

Black frogs, dollops of old truck
grease on stone pallets,
look withered and burnt
where a thin river threads its forever—

Tin tear torn from a beer
can—diligence, learn some sufficiencies—
Summer stretching its hide over
our trying to be.

Some taught themselves then passed down—
Hymns?—Nouns?—
Some taught;
arctic drifts of Then, over and over—

~

The health and milk of mornings
that end in dementia—

Polished marble facade—we're deep
in there—ethereal, thinned to a plane,

shopping for weight, heft—

The energy density of empty Space

has actually been measured

and found to be valueless—
not of
no value

Walk to where the ducks winter in gangs—
Mathematics is metaphor once

you've left the world

~

There's a hotel in Oslo where Ibsen sat
for cognac
before yelling at the actors—

chairs chained to the street, salmon
on bread—rose petal

We tried to see *Mens vi venter på Godot*

but the listing turned out a misprint—

could see his skeletal tree behind stacked
chairs

heaven isn't here—statuary, parkland—it's not
here
or left before I came

~

Death threats in September
from the ward's one phone—

The one bulb in my room—

I'm tossed against two walls

to wait

Explanatory Gap

I was out. I'd been put under. White carnation
pressed to the face. They were performing an operation and outside
the tent of potted light, eyes of the newly

conscious glowed red
hovering like embers in an updraft. They'd entered
my head through a window or portal

their bladesman had cut through the orbital plate,
it was propped open on hinges of cloth tape and weights. They'd
entered the coliseum in sandals, green coverlets, skullcaps,

gloves stretched up past their elbows
the colour of drained
flesh. There was no direct sensation of pain but

a strong sense that what pain there was had been blocked, rerouted
to some neutral place, a holding tank, a cylindrical
compartment with controlled environment

and pump-filter on timer mechanism
to be unleashed
later. I imagined stainless steel surfaces and a face

reflected there. 'Well, how to describe them? Crags, cliffs, forests,
thousands of ducks, herons and all kinds of fowl with viciously
long bills, and wilderness all around. If you were to live

here you would write
a lot of splendid things that would give the public
a great deal of pleasure, but

I am not up to it.' A blue blown in Murano sheets the overhead.
Grey sleeping bag, rain-soaked, somehow folded,
gathered, packed into an acorn and its hat re-attached.

The forest without us, its cycling
rain, its cyclamen potted and dressing a sideboard. Rest
and lean into the loam of data

not subdivided and divided again, just the normal
in pieces and flowing then lost. The monitor's on, it goes
off.

The Sickness Unto Death, and Harris on The Pig. Found.

By means of this infinite form, the self wants in despair to rule over itself.

They will get three-fourths of their food in the pasture, and we need hardly say that, where clover grows as abundantly as it does, it is the cheapest food that can be fed to a pig.

But this indicates something else; that he cannot stand being himself precisely because he failed to become Caesar.

If he objects to this; if he has no liking for a refined, well-bred, well-behaved, well-formed pig, let him turn his attention to some other business.

There being here some form of reflection...he makes concessions—he is capable of that—and why?

up the pen tight during a storm. Their chief merit consists in their cheapness, each pen opens directly into the barnyard.
It would seem as though he had brought with him a legion of imps, and that seven of them had entered into each pig.

The form of this 'exposition' may strike many readers as odd. On the latter I have no opinion.

Fig. 34—ELEVATION OF MR. ROSEBURGH'S PIGGERY

People do neither the one nor the other; they shriek that help is impossible without ever taxing their minds, and afterwards they ungratefully lie. To lack possibility means that everything has become necessary or that everything

may be described as long and deep in the carcass, full in the ham, admitting of no neck, dish face, and an easy taking on of fat.

Take its philosophical terminology seriously, that is, literally. Many contemporary commentators have fallen

from Albany to Jefferson County, and about the same time some thoroughbred Yorkshires were introduced into the same neighbourhood. They are altogether superior in form, beauty, and refinement

ceases to be regarded under the aspect of spirit most in dread of nothing. It would be only too glad to be allowed to remain in there. And why not?

The general run of pigs in the grain-growing districts partake more or less of this. Such seems to have been the origin of the present

act of open defiance.

'Think, Pig!'
—SAMUEL BECKETT

Christian said the number
pattern directing me
to the pages from which
text had to be
drawn wasn't nearly
complex enough and
should be based
on some algorithmic
system so that
the process could
conceivably continue
indefinitely sort of
loop back on itself
or at least
to the point where all
text in both books
had been appropriated
and humorously
reassembled into
something he could
in good faith call
a project which might
take me years but
would leave me
in good stead with
certain people
in Buffalo, I said
Christian do you
remember Abraham
and Isaac and that
terribly sharp cleaving
instrument and
the talking shrub?

A Setting To

Get that aside. Just shift it. Ready?—
And that, clear a way, can you see,
I don't care it's old, back in, no back
in behind, we'll cut it away. From here
to about here. Not deep, so it can pull
away. Go ahead I'll hold. Fingers.
Fingers. Jesus. Keep on, back in maybe
arm's length. In by the piping, ok now
just tear. This'll come out. Pry it. It'll
snap. There now clear just heave it
out. Will it stay? Or prop it. Jam it up
against that. See. Then well undo all
of them. Old ones, scrap. Crumble like
this, or damp, all this gack. Drag it out
and I'll scrape. That, we'll go at that.
Here go. Aim and halfway it should just
there now yank no down, now—See?
See what I told you?—

YACHT

That about does it for boats:
The others are all the boats without any obvious
linking aspect, I therefore pass over those boats,
except to say they are lovely to be among
—GLYN MAXWELL

Verificationist

What's more unnerving, that the chevrons
        scored into the flesh on the brow
                constitute confusion, or that they point

                (as they seem to want to do) to a spot
        in back of the frontal lobe—a mappable locale—
that's truly, blackly stumped? Watch what

the hands do: while sketched on the scrim
        between sleep and not, her thumbs as infant
            bats snurl into the pack that clings

                to the flesh of her rising breast. Her eyelids
        want the field bisected, then want it magnified
or widened. We arrived one summer night

in the tobacco belt bearing bedrolls tied
        with twine, *bailer twine*, and slept
            in an anachronistic ditch. Morning

                shaved haze off the immigrant labour
        cattled on flatbeds that rumbled past
the quaintness of lettuce heads. In the barn

that was the principal clause our bunkhouse
        sat appended to, bats in the thousands
            hung, or scored the air in arcs, as

                we lay in the loft in tarred pants not
        wondering *what it was like*—We'd
irrigate the crop at night; I manned a valve

that had to be closed before a set of guns
                    were shifted west. He hammered on the feeder
                    pipe. He hammered on the feeder

                    pipe and I at the valve on the main
          could not close the flow, nor could I signal
back. I couldn't signal back, nor stop

what it was I was called to stop. She comes
          in wearing a summer halter top, two dogs
                    huff, lift, and shamble over to the face

                    she wears I recognize as tenderness.
          There's nothing difficult in this. Intent forks
off from the main, we hit the sheets in sheets

of force that light the darkened rows. It was dark
          where Roberto stood striking a wrench against
                    wet metal. He was from Oaxaca and wired

                    his wages home. The room's a lambent
          blue. No longer signalling he missed his wife,
he'd point and name a thing: *relámpago* 'lightning' *relámpago*...

A Berth in the Stern

From over the port side's rail, our two faces
cameo'd, cast back, cross-haired in the lenses
of a wandering armada of jellyfish. The surface's
slickness a zero on the State-of-Sea scale. No fog,
oil rigs mushrooming the northeast horizon,

spilling these rubbery spores, perhaps, that'll clog
the Baltic if they spawn. And I'm told they
will; something about unbalanced fish stocks.
Full day and a night, approximately, aboard
the *Prinsesse Ragnhild* letting the earth's curve

unspool under her hull. All that herring
and tritium encroaching on sea-level Lübeck,
we're pointed at Oslo's elevated ground.
Thirty-five-and-a-half thousand tonnes, a traffic
jam in her hold—I've never got my head around

how these gargantua *float*. Within her massive
warren is a micro-environment: '*The smell
of ship seized you by the sinuses: the smell
of something pressurized and ferociously synthetic.*'
Every threshold is a stepping over low walls

designed to trip, until habit lifts knees, marching,
under no orders, seeking air, or the casino. Both
luncheonette and pub offer brown cheese, salmon
on brown cheese, brown cheese under shrimp, or
just brown cheese. I think the Norse are funny,

and fine biathletes. In Rotterdam I asked one why
always the Finns and Swedes at International-level
hockey? 'We don't play well together. It's amusing
to watch our neighbours do this. We like skis, and
the dark in the forest. Do you know more of us

are on the plains than in our own country?'
'Norwegians like to fly?' She looked
into her glass, then around at the assembled,
'Minnesota, North Dakota, Saskatchewan,' she said.
'*Prairies*! Dust. Diaspora of the Norse.' We lifted

glasses above our heads, masts in that windless
bar on the Maas where there was too much singing.
Down below multiple car decks, under the decks
for trucks lined like pachyderms in the pachyderm
part of the ark, our berth in the stern just above

the propeller. A strip of mirror, two narrow bunks,
a geologic dark when the cabin door swung shut.
Dark like that dark we fear thought arises from,
coated in its oil, and might descend back into but
for our propulsion to talk over the engine's baleen

thrum and whine. Here was lightlessness,
an active black that eeled in the ear. Paired gifts,
we'd been given back to the world alive;
the incision of selfhood healed over, now adrift
in the wrong element, two mute, unshuttable eyes.

Scale Model

Tricked out in phantom gear, I imagined myself
        perfected, at least made better to the extent
that I wanted nothing more, and could hurt no one—
        which is when the world disappeared. Or
the world's model displayed under glass with figurines
        passing through parks and purchasing things
and boarding trains at dawn then transpiring, shattered
        or melted, receding back into the far hills
of the false. The story of Stories Connected, and I
        among them, constructed of them, a notch in the wood
of what's happened, wound down to a farce, just
        a face extemporizing the facts and making a meal
of what it had felt like to be. What had it felt like?
        I remember a latch on a low gate; a kiosk on a platform
that smelled of diesel and grease; a rowboat blown
        into reeds and the oars in the oarlocks; remember
my flesh on the flesh of another but limbs needed
        moving and the air needed stitching with words, or
just murmurs, it all demanded doing and seeing,
        removing the black box of immediacy to its place
on a shelf near a pot of dahlias gathering dust and
        dying. Alone now, in the glow of an Imperial mind,
I curl to the chilled sense of being other; am bench, bolt-
        hole, view of the Baltic coast, brother, or crayon set,
want to be implemented, bent to, used inside
        the watched life lived—

The Largest Island Off the Largest Island

I.

We stuck sticks in the lawn's hollows,
slept at sun-up, for an hour. Oilskin

and Mick jokes over Jameson on
the ferry out of Farewell, a sideways

rain slicking nubbled deck boards.
Lenses stared into the car trunk's

dark down in car bay four. Whale
flukes northwest, once, like greens

spooned from stew. Rainbows
out near Reykjavik leaned into

over the bow rail, and white
wake below, a volatile doily

torn at by sea that wants to be oil.
Frank held up the gig being

high over in Tilting, talking
the girls into photo-ops knee-deep

in bladder wrack. Switchblades
from popsicle sticks and clothespins,

we'd have tied our own flies and
hooked the vein hiking over

the second knuckle. Edge of the flat
earth. Fuego, Fogo, somewhere way

west of who fucking knows?

2.

It wasn't that bad. It wasn't bad.
We slid round the corner on goat's

feet to the Dep manned by the ginger-
haired man who resembled your father,

for Belle Gueule or Boreal, green tea
to go with the coke, and chips in tins

we can't get on this side--this side of
the bridge you were terrified of, its groans

and see-through pedestrian grates. Ice
down the pike keeping tour boats lashed

to shore under the shadow of the parliament
library no one can use. It's not as bad

as we thought. Our patterned nights filled
with *what comes next comes next*. And it did:

rancour in the tilted kitchen, kisses while
you bathed, bullying silence as the grounds

got banged into the can. Give me the chemicals,
we're not leaving for days.

3.

Paint cans with gummed lids,
buckled, and shut like bad clams.

Stir-sticks half-naked in moted
light. Particleboard and exposed

studs. The skelf of a nail bent
back, hammered down in the grain.

Washers stare like squid from a silted
jam jar. Skis lick down through

the rafters. Knot-hole the size
and swirl of an ear. A push mower

cowers under the workbench,
sniffing oil stains. A plinth

of chipped bricks near intestines
of hose that moult on a door-hook.

A dog changes gears in a hedge.
One pane rattles. He turns six.

4.

Pig in painted numbers, nosing
the low slats where straw rags,

resined brown, stroke the fairground's
polished concrete. In a papered

metal pen that keeps her fat
from crushing seven. Seven on

spikes staccato in the show
booth, snoring at their siblings'

nose-holes. Galway blacks
could jump a five-rail gate

any horse and rider'd balk at.
In transit, a school of teeth like prawn

the driver wades into wearing
chain mail. Vietnamese potbellies

petted and picked up and flung
back at the goat. Fistfuls of spilling

pellet. They move like moles.
The ribbons are satin and blue.

Run-off exits a pipe all day and
a dump truck takes it off.

5.

When he got sick, worms were
pinching the blossom petals and

pulling them underground. Moonlight
made the little flags glow, blink

out, so the night lawn shimmered
galactic. We didn't know

what was happening. The doctors
aren't given to telling; they'd dose

him and send him home to float.
A city in Japan makes a festival

of this, all brush stroke, seafood
and a divine quiet. He set about

digging his shallow moat.

The Tall Ships Docked in Kiel Harbour
FOR DON COLES

Norwegian, Russian, Polish, Estonian.
A spectral mist had curtained the port and spread,
silken, dewy, over the crowded park grounds.
Can we say *spectral* mist, or even *mist*, wasn't
it more a greased, Baltic fog? We can say
the masts appeared broken, occluded at times;
the water that slapped the low stone rampart
could be heard clearly but relied on inference
to be known to be there, or, looking back, at the very
least, the edges of things went grainy, lost
substance, and shivered; mothers with kids
in their care sampled baked sweets or nudged hand
crafts on display tables then sank away into
enveloping dampness from which cries of
where are you carried through a muffled din—
No, this would have reached us as
Wo bist du and could we really have
isolated a phrase like that, being new to a tongue?—
An area roped off for children held rough-
hewn, log play-structures, the bark left on so they
looked ribbed and reptilian; metal boxes strapped
to lamp poles spat out cigarette packs if you
thumbed in the coins. We might have thumbed
in the coins. The masts, when they split
the slate-coloured veils, leaned and rattled, or
knocked against parts of their rigging, and small
triangular flags hung limp from the upper reaches
where the masts narrowed. Gulls landed—or terns
landed—on the crosspieces where the sails were
furled and tied like camping gear. It might have
rained, as our feet were soaked through, and we wanted
not to be where we were, but felt also an internal
pressure, like a note left for oneself in a home one

has yet to move into, to *look*, to *take in* the thick
beams of each building, the docks buried in fog,
the cider smell and steam from steel vats, the layer
of beaded wetness on things and the people who
handled those things: cups, wallets, paper containers
of food, rucksacks, umbrellas, the odd camera or
brass-handled cane. The ships lumbered away, sniffing
each other's sterns; someone's future warmed into
high resolution as love's rags clapped in a weird wind.

Explanatory Gap

Wait. Hold. I was happy just then; a breeze entered in, garlanded
with creosote, cut grass, and a sharper tang that chilled it by degrees
and told me autumn's coming on—

Back then I was a kicking colt with an arrogant mane, everything
wrong with the world, I wasn't *understood*,
a town with more churches than sense, a defensive streak

that flared whenever it could; I felt no fealty but the potential for it
when the valley's trees pulled their embarrassing sports coats on
and a wind traipsed east through the funnel the Laurentians formed,

whipping the river to soft swabs of white where it'd lazed all summer.
I could smell C. where she lingered on my face;
part wine, part almond, and I want to say metallurgic, tinny,

or minerals of the earth. One wants to be in love
but moreover, one wants to be one, narratively speaking; Towers
of Tofino. Saccade. What did we miss?

Saccade. Blisterpack. Wind rose. Fill us in later.
Slate-grey iris of Olympic Stadium collapses into its pupil.
Meadowlark that banged on morning's window just one
                                    in a percussive trend.

Airstream Land Yacht

Where in the world to go, to go?
    O where in this world to go?
This big old wagon's slow, it's slow.
    My beautiful wagon's
        slow.

It shines a silver sheen, though,
    its silver sheen a-glow.
This silvery ovoid's sturdy, ho!
    metallic armadil-
        . lo.

Born in nineteen six-and-oh, and Oh,
    she's factory clean.
Awesome to behold but slow, but slow;
    she's sort of like a
        brain.

She's sort of like a model brain, no?
    Just sits there unless towed.
And a constant need to unload, to forego,
    what we couldn't take or
        know.

On Utility

A post, only just deserving the name,
grew up or appeared in the worn earth
of the quad's footpath—
it asks what top-down planning's worth.
Someone cuts out a coupon for Thanks, another
for Many Thanks. Another cuts out a coupon
for Thanks, another for Many
Thanks. Another cuts
out Many Thanks, pockets Thanks, then Many Thanks,
then stands in the room as it darkens
according to the light outside
we call Natural. It's been programmed to behave.

Because the vast warehouse space in which their days
are spent—the poured cement, the cement
floor, the door
for lunch and the barred window casement—
now seems to move under the moving
grass of sales-lot tinsel,
or instead the tinsel's
a lung's cilia through which the currents of air
normally all but absent are visible,
or the qualities are visible, or the content
of air from ducts in motion become what we're meant
to see here—
Am I Here?
I didn't build the shelter but sat in it and looked,
looked out onto the passing phantasm of exchange.
Then I built a shelter but didn't look, as
there were more discarded bottles than could easily be counted.
The bottles formed an ice floe. They formed a reservoir
and became the lake we
can no longer drink from.
Rain became steel; became little pellets of perfectly

round, Newtonian weather precipitating
giggles and a species of quiet
anguish. Was that too much?
They find their level.

Does anyone connect looking
anymore with beauty? While the tall ships moored in slots
transmit morse to the positioned storm-
lights, a friend leaves his squat
and happens onto, or falls into—
while picking bottles—a web. A workbook. No, a web.
No, a workbook of white, and what white is there isn't Blank
but put there as white, as work, as what
we do with hours
and ask to be paid.
He clipped out Thanks, pocketed Many Thanks. He picked
up photos, on a corner of the dragging phantasm, of no one
and returned them to no one by land mail, as record
of having been: *I was Here*—
You weren't. It was a record of having been,
or of anguish. I no longer speak to him.

Water levels fell,
an obliterative cloud of Doings loomed. I mean, there was a threat,
but I'd attached, just beneath me, and for the duration, a name.
I'd attached my name
to a plate then attached the plate to me, where I
sat in the shelter, or lit kiosk, looking out.
It *was* a web; a white web spanning the cement struts
that prop up the overpass.
He slept there.
We were talking about the movement of air: billowing
white air, smoke translated from the thrashing
key strokes; a turnstile spins according

to the force of wind; smoke from the friction
of wooden dowels knitting
the unused threads together:
A patchwork version of future—
A blankness that isn't vision—
After burying myself in boreal dirt, then digging that self out,
I carried a stone around wherever I went, though
a stone the size of my head, I found, wasn't
my head. No loose threads showed. Or loose threads
showed we chose to ignore faced
with the heat of winter. What's
here, now, for a time
was something else entirely.

Jerome's Rock

Sort of crescent-shaped, grey granite, canted
at an angle, like the metal bed
a trailer hitches
into just behind its cab

but plopped at the perihelion of a crescent
beach where driftwood timber
changes its
arrangement with each tide.

Sand-flea'd kelp wigs blacken; braided
and crisp. A weir at the mouth
of the bay being
figured out by seals whose whiskered

sneers submarinely ignore warning shots
from a propane cannon. They close
their ears. It was here,
on this rock, in eighteen-ninety-something

villagers found a man starfished, famished,
rolling his eyeballs at the sky.
Parched to a papery
cut-out. Both legs had been surgically

removed. Above the knee. Arteries cinched
tight or clamped or cauterized so
a sub-promethean amount
of blood hardened in the sand to French

dessert. They took him in—the locals did—
staunched whatever leaked, bandaged,
balmed, and watered
this 'Jerome' the Fundy waters didn't want.

They weren't not funny back then either;
'Who's buoy is this?' 'How'd Jerome
here on those?'
and a winter's worth of 'Bob'

jokes. He lived out his days here, a fixture
first in Sandy Cove, then further
down the shore
among Acadians, not once revealing origins,

family name, or what happened to his limbs.
When I've fanned out
the glossy colour
prints of that place, the rock's not there.

Shots from the rock looking east toward
the weir, that part of the beach;
shots of her
on the sand to the west where

a fishhouse on a wharf exposes bleached
flanks, that's all there. But
history sits
about where my own wrinkled stare

looks out at gill-netters, heat haze, the horizon
spitting at the spot where I want
a whale to appear,
or would want if I were still there.

Compatibilist

Awareness was intermittent. It sputtered.
              And some of the time you were seen
                        asleep. So trying to appear whole

                        you asked of the morning: Is he free
              who is not free from pain? It started to rain
a particulate alloy of flecked grey; the dogs

wanted out into their atlas of smells; to pee
              where before they had peed, and might
                        well pee again—though it isn't

                        a certainty. What is? In the set,
              called Phi, of all possible physical worlds
resembling this one, in which, at time t,

was written 'Is he free who is not free—'
              and comes the cramp. Do you want
                        to be singular, onstage, praised,

                        or blamed? I watched a field of sun-
              flowers dial their ruddy faces toward
what they needed and was good. At noon

they were chalices upturned, gilt-edged,
              and I lived in that same light but felt
                        alone. I chose to phone my brother,

                        over whom I worried, and say so.
              He whispered, lacked affect. He'd lost
my record collection to looming debt. I

forgave him—through weak connections,
                through buzz and oceanic crackle—
                        immediately, without choosing to,

                        because it was him I hadn't lost; and
                later cried myself to sleep. In that village
near Dijon, called Valley of Peace,

a pond reflected its dragonflies
                over a black surface at night, and
                        the nuclear reactor's far-off halo

                        of green light changed the night sky
                to the west. A pony brayed, stamping
a hoof on inlaid stone. The river's reeds

lovely, but unswimmable. World death
                on the event horizon; vigils with candles
                        in cups. I've mostly replaced my records,

                        and acted in ways I can't account for.
                Cannot account for what you're about
to do. We should be held and forgiven.

Notes on the Poems

The epigraph to the first section is from "The Auroras of Autumn" by Wallace Stevens (*The Collected Poems of Wallace Stevens*, Vintage Books, 1990).

The italicized lines in "Essentialist" are from Ralph Waldo Emerson's essay *Nominalist and Realist*. From emersoncentral.com.

The epigraph to the second section is from the story "Chance" by Alice Munro (*Runaway*, Penguin Canada, 2004).

"Miles of Europe went by, and then it was dark": The title is a sentence from the story "The Road to Santiago de Compostela" by André Alexis (*Despair, and Other Stories of Ottawa*, McClelland and Stewart, 1998).

The epigraph to the third section is from *Anton Chekhov: A Life in Letters* (Penguin Classics, 2004).

"The World's Hub": I'm entirely indebted to Martin Bennett's beautiful translation from the Italian as published in *The Faber Book of 20th Century Italian Poems* edited by Jamie McKendrick (Faber and Faber, 2004). My transplanted version also contains lyrics by Joel Gibb of The Hidden Cameras—possibly misheard.

The italicized lines in "A Berth in The Stern" are from Martin Amis's short story "Heavy Water" (*Heavy Water*, Vintage Canada, 2000).

The epigraph to the fourth section is from "The Flotilla" by Glyn Maxwell (*The Breakage*, Faber and Faber, 1998).

"On Utility": My intention was to translate the Canadian artist Germaine Koh's approach or methodology for the making of her art (insofar as I understood it) into a generative strategy for poetry. Subsequently, her own works take on the same role here as the materials of the world seem to do in her installations. The interested reader and/or art lover should visit www.germainkoh.com.

Acknowledgements

Thanks to the editors of each of the following, where many of the poems first appeared: *Maisonneuve, Brick, Exile, Fiddlehead, ARC, The Capilano Review, New American Writing* (US), *Karogs* (Latvia), *Open Field: 30 Contemporary Canadian Poets* (Persea Books, New York), and *The New Canon* (Vehicule Press, Montreal). "On Utility" was commissioned for *Germaine Koh Works* (Kunstlerhaus Bethanien, Berlin).

Assistance from The Ontario Arts Council and The Canada Council for the Arts was invaluable during the writing of this book.

Close friends read these poems and made them better. Where the poems are not better is where I wouldn't listen. I thank David O'Meara, Karen Solie, Adam Sol, and Laura Repas for their attention and generosity.

My editor, Srikanth Reddy, reengineered the gasping machine I'd made. It's more streamlined and mobile because of him.

About the Author

Ken Babstock is the author of *Mean,* which won the Atlantic Poetry Prize and The Milton Acorn People's Poet Award, and *Days into Flatspin,* winner of a K. M. Hunter Award. His poems have won Gold at the National Magazine Awards, been anthologized in Canada and the United States, and translated into Dutch, Serbo-Croatian, and Latvian. He lives in Toronto, Canada.